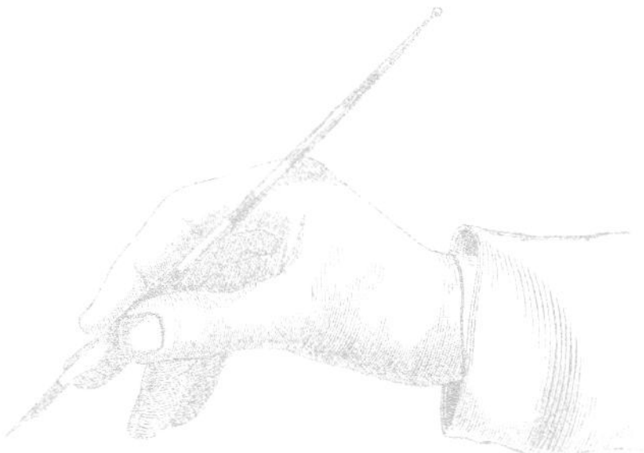

"To the world you may be one person, but to one person you are the world."

In Every Thought

Gaurav Singh

In Ever Thought

Foreword

There are many ways love enters our lives—sometimes loudly, sometimes quietly, and sometimes in ways so subtle we don't realize its power until it is gone. This book was born from those moments: the falling, the breaking, the questioning, and, finally, the healing. It is a journey not of one heart alone, but of every heart that has ever dared to feel deeply.

Poetry is not always about answers. Often, it is about holding a question long enough to hear what silence has to say. These poems do not try to solve the mysteries of love; instead, they try to sit with them—to honor the joy, the ache, the confusion, and the quiet rebirth that love always leaves behind.

You may not find yourself in every line, but you may find yourself in a pause, in an unfinished thought, in a question that has lingered in your own chest. That is the beauty of poetry: it belongs as much to the reader as it does to the writer.

Read these words slowly. Let them breathe. Some may feel like whispers, others like mirrors. Carry with you what resonates, and leave behind what doesn't.

Above all, let this book remind you of one truth: love, in all its forms, even when it ends, even when it hurts, is never wasted.

— Gaurav Singh

Preface

This book is not a story of one love, but of many. Some of these poems were written from the depths of longing, others from the edge of heartbreak, and still others from the quiet peace that follows after. Together, they form a map of emotions we all walk through when we choose to love—whether it ends with togetherness, with distance, or with silence.

I have always believed that poetry finds us when we cannot find the right words ourselves. These poems came to me in fragments—in late-night thoughts, in moments of stillness, in the kind of silence that feels louder than sound. At times they were a comfort; at times they were a release. In writing them, I discovered that love is not something that vanishes when it ends. It lingers, it transforms, and it teaches us who we are when all else is stripped away.

This book is divided into four parts—Falling, Breaking, Questioning, Healing—because love itself moves through these stages. You may find yourself pausing longer in one section than another; that is natural. Each poem, each line, is meant to meet you wherever you are in your own journey.

If these words make you remember, may they remind you of the beauty in what was. If they make you ache, may they also remind you that you are not alone. And if they make you hopeful, may they encourage you to keep opening your heart, again and again.

This book is, in the end, not just mine—it belongs to anyone who has ever loved deeply and lost, to anyone who still believes in the quiet miracle of love, even when it hurts.

— Gaurav Singh

Acknowledgments

Acknowledgment— I want to express my deepest gratitude to those who have inspired this journey—
to the readers, the dreamers, and even the silent voices
that remind us of love's depth and persistence.

To my friends and family, who patiently encouraged me
to write my heart onto the page, and to everyone
who believes in the quiet power of words.

And most of all, to the one who unknowingly shaped this story—
your presence, your absence, your laughter, your silence,
all of it lives within these pages.

* * *

Prologue

Love is many things. It is fire and water, a storm and a lull. It arrives without warning, shifts without reason, and sometimes departs without explanation. It teaches us to feel too much, to hope too much, and to grieve too much—but in its own mysterious way, it teaches us who we are.

This collection is an exploration of that journey. It moves through the exhilaration of falling, the ache of breaking, the confusion of questioning, and the quiet grace of healing. Each poem is a snapshot of a feeling, a fragment of memory, or a whisper of thought that lingered long after the moment passed.

Some poems are short, capturing a fleeting glance or a single heartbeat. Others stretch across pages, unfolding slowly like a conversation with the self or with the absence of someone we once held close. In these lines, you may recognize your own experiences, your own questions, your own quiet celebrations and sorrows.

This book is not a story with a neat ending. It is a mirror of love itself—messy, tender, painful, and ultimately transformative. May it meet you where you are, and in its reflections, may you find a piece of yourself.

Introduction

Love is not always loud. Sometimes, it exists in whispers,
in the quiet moments when no one is looking.
It lives in memories, in longing, in the ache of absence,
and in the small, invisible ways we carry someone in our hearts.

This novel is written from the perspective of a boy
who has loved, who continues to love,
and who has learned that the depth of love
cannot always be measured by presence or return.

It is my hope that these pages remind you
that love is persistent, even in silence,
and that the heart has a capacity to grow,
to endure, and to cherish endlessly.

* * *

Chapter 1

Her Silence Speaks—

I have come to understand that loving someone quietly is different from what people call "love" in stories or movies. It is not about holding hands in the rain or exchanging vows under the moonlight. It is not about fireworks or melodramatic confessions. It is about the subtle weight she carries in your chest, the way her presence infiltrates every thought, every fleeting emotion. Even when she isn't there, she is everywhere.

"Sometimes, I think love is less about holding her hand and more abo holding her presence in my heart."

I wonder if she knows how loud her silence is to me. I wonder if she has any idea how every word unsaid, every glance fleeting or unnoticed, becomes a lifetime of reflection for me. Perhaps she doesn't know. Perhaps she never will.

The quietest moments are the ones that speak the loudest. I sit alone, listening to the ordinary sounds of life—the hum of the street, the rustle of leaves, the distant laughter of strangers—and in each sound, I find her echoes. She has become my gravity. Even the most mundane moments orbit her somehow.

I try to explain this to someone, anyone, but words fail. How do you explain that someone can inhabit your heart more than your own pulse? That a single thought of her can make your day lighter, yet heavy all at once? That loving someone quietly, invisibly, is both the most exquisite and the most torturous experience you can endure?

"Love is not always in grand gestures; sometimes it is in quiet persiste in endless thought, in the heart that cannot rest."

I speak to you, reader, because there is no one else who will understand the way she does—or rather, the way I feel her. I cannot tell her; I do not dare. And yet, if I cannot speak it to her, I will speak it to someone, to anyone who will listen. Because silence, unshared, can become unbearable.

She is not perfect. She is not flawless. But she is everything to me. Her laughter, subtle and fleeting, lingers in my ears long after it has vanish

The way she tilts her head when she is thinking; the way her eyes catch the light and reflect something ineffable that I cannot describe. She is a combination of contradictions, and yet somehow, she makes sense in a world that feels entirely senseless without her.

And I love her quietly. I love her in a way that cannot be measured by time, by gestures, by recognition. I love her in the infinitesimal spaces between words, in the breaths I take when I think of her, in the moments I exist entirely because she exists.

"To love silently is to hold eternity in a single heartbeat."

Sometimes, I imagine conversations with her in my mind. I say things I will never say aloud. I confess things that have no audience except the stillness of my own heart. I imagine her smiling, tilting her head, laughing softly. I imagine her understanding me without explanation, and in these imagined moments, I feel as though I have truly loved her.

I have tried to count the ways I love her, but the list is infinite. Every thought of her births another thought, another memory, another fragment of feeling. And every fragment is precious. Even the ache that accompanies longing is a gift, because it is proof that I have loved, that I continue to love, even in the absence of acknowledgment.

Her absence is a paradox. I feel it profoundly, yet she is never truly absent. Even when she is far, even when she does not speak my name, I carry her with me. She has left traces in every corner of my consciousness, in the spaces between my words, in the subtle rhythm of my heartbeat. She is the quiet in the storm, the calm that is impossible to ignore.

"She is everywhere I go and everything I see, and still I have not begun to know the depth of her impact on me."

Sometimes I wonder if anyone else experiences love this way. A love that is not demonstrated by physical proximity or grand declarations, but by the ceaseless internal presence of someone who has touched your soul so profoundly that their absence feels like a tangible weight.

And in that realization, I find both solace and despair. Solace because I know I have loved truly, deeply, and unconditionally. Despair because I know this love may never be returned, may never be acknowledged, may remain forever confined to the quiet chambers of my heart.

I do not wish for her to return my love—not yet, perhaps, not ever. I simply wish for her to exist, even at a distance, even in a form that is not mine to claim. Because to love someone is not always to possess them; sometimes it is to honor their existence in your life, to let them occupy your heart without expecting anything in return.

"Love is not ownership; it is the sacred act of holding someone in your heart without asking for a single thing."

And so I sit, alone, and feel her. Every thought, every memory, every fleeting image of her mind's eye, consumes me entirely. And I am grateful for it. I am grateful for the quiet, for the ache, for the presence that never truly leaves.

This is how I love her. Quietly, endlessly, without expectation. And perhaps, this is enough—for now, for always, until the world changes or until I am capable of expressing in words what my heart already knows.

She is the silence that speaks to me louder than any voice ever could. She is the constant in the chaos, the stillness in the storm, the whisper in my mind that reminds me I am alive because she is remembered. And in that, I find the meaning of love.

"In her silence, I hear the symphony of my own heart, and it plays only for her."

—-

Chapter 2

The Little Things—

"It is in the little things that the heart discovers the infinite."

There is a quiet poetry in observing her, in noticing patterns that others would never see. The way her hair catches the sunlight, revealing threads of gold that seem to laugh along with her; the way her laughter, soft and unassuming, can shift the weight of my day, lifting the shadows that cling to me. It is not just her appearance, nor her words, but the way she exists in the world that captivates me.

I find myself recalling moments I never told her mattered to me. A glance, a fleeting touch, a shared silence—they are etched in my memor like delicate brushstrokes on a canvas. I remember how she tilts her he when she listens, as if the world itself has slowed so she can understanc I remember the way she hums under her breath when she is content, a quiet melody that lingers in the corners of my mind long after the moment has passed.

"The smallest gestures can speak the loudest truths of love."

Sometimes I imagine telling her all of these things, confessing every detail I have noticed, every thought that has been born from her presence. But I don't. I keep these confessions hidden, nestled in the quiet chambers of my heart. It is a strange, wonderful form of devotion—loving someone so completely that even the smallest aspect of their being becomes sacred to you.

I notice the way she pauses when she reads, as if absorbing not just the words but the meaning behind them. I notice the subtle tension in her shoulders when she worries, the way her eyes soften when she sees someone in need. Every detail is a thread that weaves her into the fabric of my life, even if she does not realize it.

"To see someone truly is to love them in ways they cannot imagine."

I love the way she is unaware of her power over me. She does not realize that a single smile can illuminate my darkest thoughts. She does not know that the mere sound of her name spoken aloud in my mind brings a warmth that spreads through my chest. I have never told her these things; perhaps I never will. And yet, my love thrives in this quiet awareness, in the intimacy of unspoken admiration.

Sometimes, I imagine conversations that could never happen. I speak to her in my mind, telling her how I feel, what I see, how deeply I am moved by the subtleties of her being. I imagine her laughing at my clumsy words, rolling her eyes at my awkward attempts, and yet smiling in a way that makes me feel understood, even in my imagination.

"I love her not for the things she does, but for the way she makes the world feel alive around her."

Even when we are apart, the small things remain with me. A fragment of her voice, a glimpse of her expression, a memory of her touch—they haunt me beautifully. I find her in unexpected places: the curl of smoke rising from my coffee, the rhythm of footsteps echoing in the hallway, the way light falls on a familiar street corner. She is everywhere, in everything, and I am endlessly captivated.

I confess to you, reader, that it is these details that sustain me. They are proof that love is not a fleeting passion, not a dramatic surge, but a persistent, quiet force that shapes the very way we perceive the world. To notice, to remember, to carry these small things in the heart is to love completely.

There is a sacredness in this kind of love. I have written little notes in my head, never sent, never shared, detailing all the minutiae of her presence that make life richer:

"The way you pause when you think, the way your eyes light up when you laugh, the softness in your voice when you speak to someone who needs it—these things are the stars that guide my heart."

I love her in ways that cannot be seen, in ways that may never beunderstood. Andperhapsthatisthepurestformoflove: to give completely without expectation, to treasure every imperceptible moment, every nuance, every tiny fragment of a person who has captured your heart so wholly.

"To love quietly is to live inside someone's essence without disturbing their world."

Even now, as I write to you, I feel her in my thoughts, shaping my world in ways no one else could. She has become the measure of beauty, the standard of joy, the quiet rhythm that keeps me anchored. And though I may never express all of this to her, it does not diminish its significance. It only deepens it, makes it more intimate, more sacred.

I sometimes fear that my love, so tied to the smallest things, will be dismissed or forgotten. But I have learned that love does not require recognition; it requires attention. It requires presence, even in absence. It requires seeing, really seeing, and holding those glimpses in the heart.

"The depth of love is measured not by words spoken, but by the quiet understanding of a soul."

And so I continue to observe, to notice, to love in the details. Every smile, every glance, every subtle inflection of her voice becomes a part of me, a part of my ongoing devotion. In this way, she is not just a person I love—she is the lens through which I see the world, the quiet light that illuminates everything around me.

Even in the small things, she teaches me what it means to love completely, unconditionally, and without expectation. And I carry her everywhere, always, finding new fragments to cherish, new details to marvel at, new reasons to love her even more.

“In every subtlety, in every quiet gesture, I find the endlessness of my love for her.

Chapter 3

The Unspoken Words—

"Some truths are too fragile for the world, yet too vital to remain silent."

I think about her constantly, and with each thought, a thousand unsaid words form in my mind. Words like "I see you," "I notice you," "You matter to me more than I can ever explain." But I never speak them aloud. Perhaps because I fear they will be misunderstood, or perhaps because speaking them might alter the fragile balance of my own devotion.

There are moments when I imagine telling her everything. I imagine sitting across from her in a quiet room, the sunlight brushing her face and I finally letting my heart pour out. I would tell her how her prese has shaped me, how her laughter is a balm to my darkest thoughts, ho her eyes hold a world I can never fully understand but always wish to explore. And yet, when I try to picture it, the words crumble in my mouth, leaving only a hollow ache behind.

"To love is to hold your tongue when your heart begs to speak."

I fear that if I reveal everything, it might be too much. That my devoti so deep and consuming, might frighten her or overwhelm her. So I ke my words buried, like seeds waiting for a season that may never come I confess them in my mind, in fragments of imagined conversations, i letters I will never send. They live in the quiet spaces of my day, in the moments when no one is watching, when the world feels still enough to contain them.

Sometimes, I whisper them to myself at night, in the darkness of my room, hoping the walls might carry them to her somehow. "I love you I say softly, almost like a prayer. "I love you even in your absence. I lo you even when you do not know it." These words have no audience, y they give me a strange sense of relief, as though by speaking them in secret, I honor the love I hold for her.

"There is courage in unspoken words; there is power in silent devotion

I have never told her about the nights I have lain awake, thinking of every nuance of her being. About how her laugh echoes in my mind lo after it is gone. About how I have memorized the subtle ways she mov the expressions she makes, the little rhythms that are uniquely hers. I have never told her how her absence makes the world feel incomplete, how her mere memory can sustain me in moments of despair.

Every unspoken word is a testament to the depth of my love. I do not withhold them out of indifference or fear of vulnerability—they are held because they are sacred. They belong to a space between us, a realm where my heart can speak freely without the risk of rejection or misunderstanding. And in this sacred space, my love flourishes, pure and untainted.

"To love silently is to protect the soul of what you hold dear."

Yet, there are times when the silence becomes unbearable. The weight of all that remains unsaid presses against me, making each breath feel heavy, each thought tinged with longing. I ache to share these truths, to let her know the extent to which she has transformed my existence. But every time I consider it, I hesitate, because words, once spoken, cannot be taken back.

And so I write to you instead, dear reader. I confess my unspoken words here, hoping that in expressing them, I might release some of the weight they carry. I tell you that she is everything to me—more than anyone could understand, more than anyone could ever deserve. I tell you that my heart beats for her, silently, unconditionally, without expectation.

"Some loves are not meant to be declared aloud; they are meant to be felt in every heartbeat."

There are nights when I imagine her reading these words, somehow knowing what I cannot bring myself to say. I picture her smiling softly, perhaps shaking her head at my sentimentality, yet understanding the depth of what I feel. And in those imagined moments, I am content, for my love has been acknowledged in the only way I can permit myself: quietly, intimately, wholly.

I sometimes wonder if she ever suspects the extent of my devotion. Does she know that my thoughts are perpetually tethered to her? Does she realize that my days, my joys, my sorrows, are all quietly influenced by the shadow of her presence? Perhaps she does, perhaps she does not. And it does not matter, because my love exists independently of her awareness.

"True love does not demand recognition; it simply persists."

I have also kept from her the ways in which her absence has shaped me. The longing, the ache, the moments of reflection that force me to confront my own fears, weaknesses, and desires. Loving her has made me vulnerable in ways I never anticipated. It has stripped me bare, leaving me exposed to the full intensity of my emotions. And yet, I would not trade it for anything, because through this vulnerability, I have discovered the profound capacity of my own heart.

Even now, as I write these words to you, I feel her close, not physically, but in every thought, every recollection, every imagined whisper. She is the silent current that carries me through each day, the invisible force that shapes my perspective, my emotions, my very being. And though I may never voice all that I feel to her directly, I know that these unspoken words define the essence of my love.

"To love in silence is to love with all that you are, without reservation, without demand."

And so I continue, carrying these unspoken words like treasures, hidden but precious, fragments of my soul offered quietly to the universe. I may never speak them aloud to her, but they exist, and they endure, as steadfast as the beating of my heart, as constant as the pull of the tides.

In the quiet moments of my day, I revisit them, relive them, hold them close. And in doing so, I find a strange peace, a recognition that love, even unspoken, is never wasted. It is not diminished by silence; it is sanctified by it.

"Even in silence, love speaks volumes to those who are willing to listen."

I write to you now, knowing that perhaps my words will reach no one, that perhaps they will vanish into the ether. But I also know that in writing them, I honor the depth of my own heart, the truth of my devotion, and the sacredness of what it means to love someone so completely, so unreservedly, without expectation or demand.

And so I wait, silently, patiently, carrying these unspoken words with me, hoping that someday, somehow, they will find their place—either within her understanding or within the quiet chambers of my own heart where they have always belonged.

"Some words are never spoken, yet they echo eternally within the soul.

Chapter 4

The Ache of Loving—

"Love is not always a solace; sometimes it is the heaviest burden one can bear."

I have tried to distract myself, to fill the emptiness with mundane tasks, with fleeting conversations, with laughter that does not reach my eyes. Yet, in every attempt, her presence finds a way back into my consciousness. A memory, a fragment of her smile, the way her voice sounded in passing—all of it resurfaces with cruel precision, reminding me of what I have lost and what I cannot possess.

There is an irony in this ache: it is proof of the depth of my love, yet it isolates me from the world. People see me, but they do not see her in me. They cannot perceive the subtle ways she has become a part of my existence, how every thought, every breath, every heartbeat carries traces of her. And so I suffer quietly, silently, unseen and yet profoundly moved by the shadow of her presence.

"The deepest loves are often the loneliest, for they exist largely in the unseen corners of the heart."

Some nights, the ache is unbearable. I lie awake, staring at the ceiling, imagining her somewhere else, living a life in which I may not exist. And the thought is both a knife and a balm: it cuts through the illusions I hold, yet it reminds me that I am capable of loving so intensely, so purely, that the absence of its object cannot diminish it.

I have learned to measure my days not by the passing hours, but by the moments when her presence pierces the veil of distance. A glance remembered, a laugh recalled, a fleeting thought of her walking down a street I am not on—all of these are threads that tie me to her, threads I clutch desperately, even when they wound me.

"To love someone in their absence is to carry both joy and sorrow in the same heartbeat."

I sometimes question myself. Why do I continue to love when the world insists she is gone? Why do I invest so much of my being into someone who may never return it? And yet, the answers are simple. Love, in its purest form, is not transactional. It does not require reciprocity. It is a force that shapes the lover, even more than the beloved. And in loving her, I have discovered depths of myself I did not know existed.

I have tried to imagine a world where I could forget her, where I could move on, where her absence did not ache so deeply. But the more I attempt to let go, the more impossible it becomes. She is woven into the fabric of my life. Every thought, every decision, every fleeting feeling carries her mark. And even if she never returns, even if the world forgets her, I cannot.

"The heart remembers what the mind wishes it could forget."

And so, I endure. I endure the ache, the longing, the bittersweet weight of loving someone who is not here. I endure because it is part of who I am. I endure because love, in its quiet persistence, teaches patience, resilience, and the ability to find beauty even in suffering.

Sometimes, I imagine her smiling at another, hearing her laughter in a place I cannot be, and I feel a pang so sharp it cuts through me. And yet, I do not resent her. I do not wish her absence had never happened, nor do I wish she had never existed. I only wish I could convey the immensity of my feelings, to let her know that even from afar, even in silence, my heart is entirely hers.

"To love beyond reach is to understand the depth of devotion itself."

Even in my solitude, I find moments of strange grace. The ache reminds me that I am alive, that my capacity to feel is not diminished by absence. It shapes my days, colors my thoughts, and deepens my reflections.

Loving her is a discipline, a constant practice of emotional endurance and quiet adoration.

There are times when I walk the streets and see couples, friends, laughter, and I feel a hollow ache in my chest. Yet, I also feel a warmth that comes from knowing that my love is untainted by expectation. It is a pure devotion, entirely mine, entirely sacred. And though it is painful, it is also beautiful.

"Love is both the wound and the salve, the ache and the delight, inseparable and eternal."

I have learned to channel this ache into reflection, into self-growth, into understanding the vast complexity of my own heart. I examine why I feel so deeply, why her absence strikes me so profoundly, and what it teaches me about desire, attachment, and the endurance of love. And through this process, I become not only more aware of her, but of myself.

Even as I write these words, I feel her near, not in body, but in essence. She has imprinted herself onto my soul so deeply that her absence cannot erase her. And though my heart aches daily, though each thought of her is a mixture of longing and pain, I continue. Because to cease loving would be to cease living in the way I have come to know myself.

"In loving her, I have learned the expanse of my own heart, and the depth of the human spirit."

And so I endure. I endure the ache, I endure the absence, and I endure the endless thoughts of her that occupy my every waking moment. I endure because love is not a fleeting comfort—it is a lifetime, a constant, a force that shapes us whether we wish it to or not.

Even in the heaviest moments, I find solace in knowing that loving her, with all its pain and beauty, is a testament to the capacity of the heart to feel beyond reason, beyond reciprocity, beyond time.

"To love is to live fully, even when the one you love is gone

Chapter 5

Memories in the Quiet

—

"Memories are the softest echoes of love, lingering long after the moment has passed."

I remember the first time I truly noticed her—not in a dramatic way, not with fireworks or poetry, but in a simple, ordinary moment that became extraordinary in retrospect. I remember the way she smiled at something insignificant, how her eyes crinkled, and how the world seemed to pause, letting me savor the smallest details. I did not know then that these seemingly trivial moments would anchor me to her in ways I could never have imagined.

Sometimes, I relive the laughter we shared, small private jokes that only existed between us. Those memories are bright with warmth, yet tinged with the ache of absence. Every detail—the sound of her laugh, the way her hand brushed mine by accident, the way she would look at me when she thought I wasn't watching—feels like a lifetime packed into a single frame. I clutch these memories as though they were fragile glass, afraid to let them slip, afraid to lose her again in the endless flow of time.

"Even the smallest shared moments become eternal in the heart of someone who loves deeply."

I remember the quiet evenings we spent together, speaking about nothing and everything. The world outside ceased to exist. Our conversations were not always profound; sometimes we spoke in trivialities, yet every word carried significance because it was shared. I remember thinking, even then, how rare it was to feel such intimacy without needing grandeur or theatrics. Love, I realized, could exist in simplicity, in the comfort of being near someone who understands you without effort.

There are memories of gentle conflicts too, small disagreements that ended in laughter or shared understanding. Even the moments of tension carry their own tenderness, because they reminded me that love is not just about joy—it is about connection, about navigating life together, about caring enough to care when things are difficult. I have come to treasure every memory, every nuance, because they are pieces of a puzzle that formed the shape of our shared existence.

“Memories are not just reminders of the past; they are bridges that connect our hearts across time and distance.”

I sometimes imagine her reading my thoughts, hearing the silent words I never spoke. I wonder if she remembers these moments the way I do, or if they exist only in my memory, vivid and unrelenting. Does she think of me at all, I ask myself, or have my footprints faded in the sands of her consciousness? It does not matter, for the memories themselves are enough to sustain me. They are proof that love, once lived, leaves a permanent mark on the soul.

I remember her eyes, bright and searching, filled with curiosity and empathy. I remember her voice, soft and melodic, capable of soothing and challenging in equal measure. I remember how she made even ordinary days feel sacred. These memories are not static; they live and breathe within me, coloring my present, shaping my thoughts, and inspiring my reflection.

“The past lives in us, not as shadow, but as light guiding the way forward.”

Sometimes I am overwhelmed by the realization that all these memories, vivid as they are, cannot bring her back. I cannot touch her, speak to her, or relive the moments in reality. And yet, I do not resent this. For even in absence, the memories remind me of the capacity of my heart to feel, to hold, and to endure. They are a testament to the love that was, and that continues to be in subtle, invisible ways.

I recall the quiet moments we shared in parks, in coffee shops, in empty streets at dusk. Our hands might have brushed, our shoulders might have touched, and the world did not notice, but I did. I noticed everything. Every glance, every gesture, every breath was a message, a sign of connection that needed no words. And now, in their absence, these moments are treasures I carry alone, sacred relics of a love that shaped me.

"Even in silence, memory preserves the most profound expressions of love."

I think about how these memories influence me even now. They make me more attentive, more aware of the beauty in small gestures, more sensitive to the quiet joys that life offers. Loving her, and remembering her, has taught me patience, gratitude, and reverence for the little things. And even though she is gone, these lessons remain, embedded in my consciousness, shaping my character, guiding my heart.

Sometimes, I speak to her in my mind, walking through these memories as though she were beside me. I tell her that I remember, that I honor what we shared, that I carry her in the deepest parts of myself. And even if she never knows, even if these words never reach her, I feel a strange peace. For love is not measured solely by presence or reciprocity—it is measured by the depth of feeling, the constancy of care, and the reverence with which one preserves the past.

"Memories are the vessels of love that time cannot diminish."

I continue to relive the quiet laughter, the gentle touches, the shared silences. They are my refuge, my solace, my connection to something eternal. And in these moments, I understand that love does not end with absence, nor with loss. It persists, it endures, it lives within us, shaping us in ways that are invisible but undeniable.

Even in solitude, I find her. Even in the most ordinary moments, I am reminded of what we had. And though I cannot change the past, I carry it forward, letting it inform my present, guiding my thoughts, nurturing my heart, and reminding me that love, once it has touched your soul, never truly leaves.

“In the quiet of memory, love remains vivid, eternal, and unbroken.

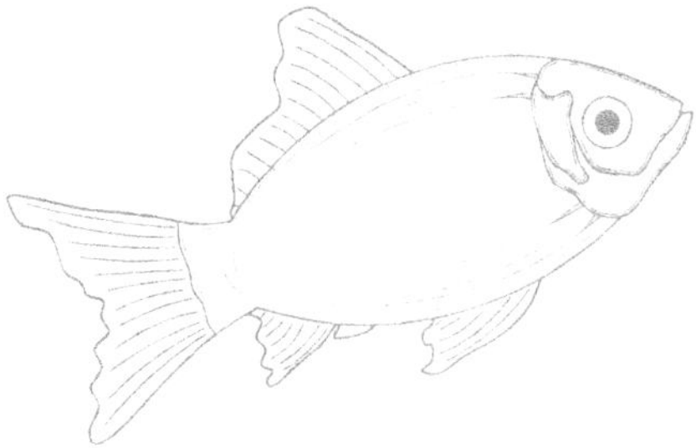

Chapter 6

Confessions in the Quiet

—

I I have with others, in the quiet corners of my own mind.
Loving her has become a lifelong rhythm, a pulse I cannot turn off, a song I cannot stop humming.

"Some loves are not meant to be spoken, only lived."

I admit to you, reader, that I have tried. I have tried to move on, to fill the emptiness with other things, other people, other distractions. But every attempt ends the same way: with her. She is the lens through which I see the world, the benchmark of joy and warmth, the measure of what it means to feel deeply. I cannot erase her from my life, nor would I want to.

Every day, I wake with the memory of her and go to sleep with it. And in between, I live a quiet, subtle devotion that no one else can see. I love her not for what she gives, not for what she returns, but simply because I cannot do otherwise. Loving her has become as natural as breathing, as inevitable as the passage of time.

"To love is to continue, even when the world has moved on."

I have reflected on the boy I was when I first met her and the man I am becoming. Loving her has changed me in ways I cannot fully articulate. It has taught me patience, humility, and the beauty of selfless devotion. I have learned that love is not about possession; it is about reverence, about cherishing someone without expectation, about finding meaning in the very act of caring.

And still, I ache. I ache for the moments we could have had, for the words I never spoke, for the closeness that is now impossible. I ache because I love her more today than I did yesterday, and I know I will love her even more tomorrow. This is the paradox of unreturned love—it grows, it deepens, it transforms into something both painful and beautiful.

"The heart remembers, and with each remembering, it grows fuller, even in absence."

I confess that I think about her constantly. I imagine the life she leads now, the people she meets, the joys she experiences, and I hope—truly hope—that she is happy. Even if happiness no longer includes me, even if she has forgotten the tenderness we once shared, I cannot wish her anything but light. For loving her has taught me compassion beyond myself, the capacity to care for her as a separate being, not just as someone who fulfills my desires.

Yet, in my quiet confessions, I make a vow to myself: I will continue to grow, to become the boy worthy of loving her—even if that love is never reciprocated. I will take each day as a chance to improve, to be better, to hold onto the qualities that made her love me once and might make her see me again—not because I demand it, but because I am learning to embody it fully.

"Love is not always about winning someone over; sometimes it is about becoming the best version of yourself because of them."

I confess, too, that I am afraid. Afraid of forgetting her, afraid of allowing life to dull the intensity of what I feel, afraid that the ache might fade into something less meaningful. But I remind myself that love does not diminish with absence. It does not weaken with time. It transforms. It becomes a quiet strength, a force that shapes your choices, your reflections, your understanding of yourself.

And so I live in the quiet, holding her in my heart, cherishing the memories, honoring the absence, and nurturing the love that endures. I confess this to you, dear reader, because perhaps in sharing it, I can make sense of it all. Perhaps by writing it down, by giving it form in words, I can understand that love, even unreturned, is a gift.

"There is a sacredness in loving beyond hope, in holding someone dear even when they are not yours to hold."

I do not know what the future holds. I do not know if she will ever return, if she will ever know the depth of my feelings, if our paths will cross again in ways that make sense to both of us. But I do know this: I will continue to love her. I will continue to grow. I will continue to hope, in silence, in patience, in quiet devotion.

Even as I write these words, I feel her in the spaces around me. In the morning light, in the rustle of leaves, in the hum of a city that moves without pause, she is there. She is in the memories I hold, in the lessons I have learned, in the person I am becoming. Loving her has become inseparable from who I am, and I accept it fully.

"To love is not to possess, but to cherish; not to claim, but to honor; not to forget, but to carry eternally."

And so, this is my confession in the quiet. I will love her today, a little more than yesterday. I will love her tomorrow, a little more than today. And I will continue, in silence, in devotion, in reverence, because love is not always measured by the presence of the beloved—it is measured by the persistence of the heart that beats for them, endlessly, without demand or expectation.

And as the final word, as the echo that carries through the pages of this quiet love story, I leave this truth:

"Love is not about holding on, or letting go—it is about carrying someone in your heart, beautifully, relentlessly, forever."

Conclusion

-Loving someone, even in their absence, is a journey of self-discovery,
reflection, and quiet devotion.

Through these pages, I hope you have felt the depth of a heart
that continues to love despite distance and time,
and that you have been reminded of the power of memory,
the beauty in unspoken words, and the resilience of the human soul.

Love is not always about having someone by your side;
it is about carrying them within, beautifully, relentlessly,
and allowing that love to shape the person you become..

* * *

Epilogue

Love is many things. It is fire and water, a storm and a lull. It arrives without warning, shifts without reason, and sometimes departs without explanation. It teaches us to feel too much, to hope too much, and to grieve too much—but in its own mysterious way, it teaches us who we are.

This collection is an exploration of that journey. It moves through the exhilaration of falling, the ache of breaking, the confusion of questioning, and the quiet grace of healing. Each poem is a snapshot of a feeling, a fragment of memory, or a whisper of thought that lingered long after the moment passed.

Some poems are short, capturing a fleeting glance or a single heartbeat. Others stretch across pages, unfolding slowly like a conversation with the self or with the absence of someone we once held close. In these lines, you may recognize your own experiences, your own questions, your own quiet celebrations and sorrows.

This book is not a story with a neat ending. It is a mirror of love itself—messy, tender, painful, and ultimately transformative. May it meet you where you are, and in its reflections, may you find a piece of yourself

Afterword

As you reach the end of this collection, I hope you feel the echoes of every step taken through love's many landscapes—falling, breaking, questioning, and healing. These poems are not meant to provide answers, but to honor the experience of loving fully, with all its joy, confusion, and sorrow.

Love does not always follow the paths we expect. Sometimes it lingers, sometimes it leaves, and sometimes it teaches us lessons we could not have imagined. Yet in all its forms, love leaves a mark, shapes a heart, and transforms the way we see the world.

If these words have moved you, even in the smallest way, then they hav fulfilled their purpose. Carry the poems that resonated, leave behind the ones that did not, and remember: healing is not linear, grief is not shameful, and love—both past and present—always shapes who we are.

Thank you for taking this journey with me. May your heart continue to open, to feel, and to grow.

— Gaurav Singh

About the Author

Gaurav Singh is a writer who explores the depths of love, memory, and human emotion.

Through his words, he seeks to capture the quiet intensity of feelings that are often hidden from the world but resonate deeply in the heart.

When not writing, he enjoys reflecting on life, observing small details, and discovering beauty in the ordinary moments that make us human. This is his second novel, inspired by the enduring power of love.

9 789334 403039

Printed at Repro India Ltd.